W9-DDL-553

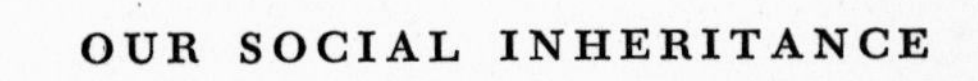

OUR SOCIAL INHERITANCE

by Clarence Irving Lewis

Our Social Inheritance

INDIANA UNIVERSITY PRESS
Bloomington

LIBRARY OF CONGRESS CATALOG CARD NUMBER: 57-7707

MANUFACTURED IN THE UNITED STATES OF AMERICA

Acknowledgment

The chapters that follow were presented as public lectures at Indiana University in the spring of 1956 under the auspices of the Mahlon Powell Foundation.

Preface

IT IS one of the plain implications of what is set down in this small book that nobody could be really competent to write it. Also, as will soon appear, it presents no facts which are not obvious and contains little which has not been said before and very likely better said. In the third place, no one could be realistic about its topic without skirting the danger of being edifying.

Believing that it is well to remind ourselves of certain obvious and gratifying facts about our social inheritance, I accept the hazards. But I make it brief. Let any reader who will, revise what I here attempt, making his own emendations and supplementations.

I should like to record the fact that what is here put forward represents a direction of thinking to which I was first drawn by Josiah Royce. If my thoughts have now strayed from the path to which his counsels pointed, still I hope he might not be displeased with them.

I have had the honor of presenting these lectures under the auspices of the Mahlon Powell Foundation at Indiana University, in May 1956, and also of their inclusion in the program of the Western Division of the American Philosophical Association meeting at the same time and place. I wish to thank both the Philosophy Department of Indiana University and the officers and members of the Western Division for the arrangement by which I have enjoyed this privilege.

C. I. LEWIS

Stanford, California
April 18, 1956

Contents

1

THE BACKGROUND

1. THE BACKGROUND

THE theme is the social inheritance of mankind, —or not more than incidentally and by implication—that of twentieth-century Americans.

"Know thyself" is a time-honored maxim. As Pope later phrased it, "The proper study of mankind is man." And these adages have their peculiar aptness by the fact that self-consciousness is indeed a distinctive mark of humankind. There is nothing in man's make-up or in the kind of life which he alone among the animals can live, or in the problems he must learn to solve, which does not take its color from the character of the human creature as reflective, self-conscious and capable of deliberation in decision, self-determining and self-critical in action.

Also from of old, men have sought to sharpen this self-understanding by comparison of themselves with other creatures, as they have observed them and supposed their conscious life to be. And the broad features of the contrast they have so been led to draw still has its force. The animal of any other species lives in the world of his own neighborhood, made familiar to him by his own experience. He sees what is presented to his eyes, hears what strikes his ear, and is warned of the impending by what is wafted to his nose. He enjoys and suffers in the present, is incited or inclined to action by what falls within the horizon of his senses, and he acts as he feels moved to do. Like ourselves, he lives in time and what he endures will leave its mark upon him; but the time he lives in passes and is gone, and the future discloses itself to him only in the dawning of it. His troubles are of the present hour, and tomorrow is for him the day that never comes.

Man consciously lives in a universe which runs beyond his measuring, and in a terrestrial epoch whose character reflects aeons of past change which he has puzzled to make out. He finds himself where he is as a result of centuries-long migrations of peoples, whose habits and modes of life he patiently reconstructs from the ashes of their campfires, the bones of other animals mingled with their own, and from the artifacts which they have left. He recognizes his descent from them and construes himself as the product of his long past in history. He consciously looks forward to the future, and finds himself moving into a period whose vicissitudes for his children and his children's children arouse his hopes and fears. It is his recognition that, in part, he has brought about these troubles, or allowed them by his mistakes and insufficient foresight, and that only he and other men can meet and solve them.

Within his own life, he is unable to live from moment to moment, responding to the here and now as the felt poignancies of it move him to do. He both can and must live in the light of the future he anticipates and with the salt and savor of his remembered past. In action, he has a range of choice unknown to any other creature, vouchsafed to him by his capacity to forecast, in measure, the future as it will be and the possible as it can be, dependent on what he may decide to bring about. By the scope of his imaginative understanding, alternative futurities are spread out before him, each needing but the touch of his decisive act to become reality. That which he chooses will be actual by his deed, and the others will be forever left in the limbo of what might have been. But by the same token the freedom of irresponsibility is lost to him. He is open to remorse for what he has brought about or what he failed to do: he cannot respond as present feeling incites him merely but must face the future with concern and act with care. What he chooses to bring about, he must thereafter recognize as his doing which he never can disown. His freedom of choice is the necessity of decision and the responsibility for what is chosen and decided. This freedom and this responsibility, whether as privilege or as burden, are a part of his inheritance as human; and the acceptance and exercise of them are the vocation of man.

Freedom of choice and responsibility for decision and for action belong to the individual in his individual living, and they belong to men together in their living together and acting together. The ethos is the social direction of social living just as the individual code of conduct is the critical and deliberate direction of the individual's self-determined doing.

It is the further character of mankind that without an interweaving of the individual with the social which, in the full scope and import of it, is unlike that of any other species, no such creature as man could have come to be. There are other animals which are social; those gramnivores which unite in herds for the common defense, the beasts of prey which hunt in packs, and those insects which approximate in some degree and some respects to the organization and the differentiations of function of the human social order. But the generations of other animals are born to the social organization which characterizes them, and the modes of behavior essential to the preservation of it are merely instinctive or result from the conditioning of infancy. Speaking in the broad—and we can only so speak here—their ways of behaving, individually and in their group reactions, persist from generation to generation as concomitant of their physical inheritance, and are modes of response which pass unchanged so long as the biological strain and the general environment remains unaltered.

By contrast, the human modes of social living show some measure of progressive modification; changes in the way of life which come about with little or no correlative alteration of the biological inheritance, and likewise in the absence of any alteration of the natural environment which would be sufficient to account for them. If there be any causal factor in external circumstances, to which a particular such alteration of the mode of life could be attributed, it is likely to be found in some change which men themselves have made in their environment—in shelters they have learned to build, or in tools which they have fashioned, or in newly discovered uses for the things about them. The ways in which men live differently and alter their activities as time goes on, and the ways in which their living together is marked by modifications in the social structure, admit of no sufficient explanation by alteration of the biological inheritance; and they are not confined to such as correlate with some uncontrollable change of the environment. If we look to living and acting as functionings of the individual organism only, then, to be sure, we may see no modification not plausibly to be accounted for by correlative differences in genetic or environmental factors. But if we look to the social phenomena, or to the intangible and the spiritual (or whatever other term you wish for that which manifests itself in modes of thought and the content of convictions and beliefs), or even if we look only to the material things which are products of our living together, then an evolution of the human, inexplicable without reference to causes which are also human, must be evident. And if we direct attention to that which is of most concern to men themselves—to the level of life attained, in terms of the satisfactions it may afford and the amelioration of its hardships—then the witness to this continuing alteration, actuated by what is internal to man himself, must be overwhelming. It is this phenomenon of self-actuated and progressive change in the modes and products of group living, in which the history of man finds no parallel in that of any other creature. Human society has, in its most telling aspects, made itself: it is something brought about by men, reacting to one another and acting together.

Particularly, this civilization which men create represents the confluence of their thinking, directed upon what they deem desirable and what they would avoid, and upon their acts addressed to purposes so arising which they hold in common. Most particularly of all, there is one factor in the absence of which no congeries of other causes would be sufficient to produce this manner of evolution which is confined to the human species. That factor is the perpetuation of whatever practices are found to be conducive to human betterment, through the operation of the social order itself

—through the social memory, as distinguished from the merely individual recollection, which animals of other species also have, of that which is experienced in the first person. It is by this agency of a group tradition, and practices inculcated with group sanction, that whatever ways of doing and behaving are adjudged to be of value for achievement of some purpose which is common are added to the store of common learning, imparted to individuals whose own experience might not otherwise suffice for the attainment of them, and passed on from one generation to the next.

The prime requisite of the human march from primitive savagery to modern civilization lies in this fact—often enough observed before—that man is the only animal which has such social memory and retains not only what has been learned from his individual experience but also what has been inculcated by the experience of generations past and of the race.

Even this most indispensable and all-important factor would not, however, be sufficient by itself to explain the continuous and progressive modification of human life. Tradition is the conserving factor—and conservative: often enough it operates to freeze the status quo and stands in the way of further modification. This marks the necessity of another factor to be observed, and one which is equal in importance: man also is the self-critical animal; he achieves some measure of self-understanding; he comes to envisage his own personal goals, and those he holds in common with other men; he discovers his own potentialities, discerns his own limitations, reflectively criticizes his own behavior, evaluates his activities by the results of them, and continually redirects himself to his critically chosen ends.

These two factors, the social memory and critical self-consciousness, represent the decisive and proximate grounds of that character of human history in which it represents a type of evolution which is unique. However, even these most potent factors could not have wrought this unparalleled result without other and more remote ones which nevertheless are essential conditions of its possibility. Among such further requisite and contributory factors there are some which are peculiar to man as a biological organism, or more directly derivative from his physical capacities. These are characteristics more patent to external observation, and the emphasis has oftentimes been placed upon them. Let us first direct attention to the more notable of such background factors. Having duly noted these, we may then return to the topic of those determinants which are decisive in the nearer sense and more explanatory.

It is a commonplace that the kind of life which man can live, as contrasted with what is possible to other creatures, is fundamentally dependent on two thing; human hands, and his more complex nervous system allowing of more complicated modes of response.

No effect which any organism can produce in the external world can come about otherwise than by the displacement of something: it moves some object from the place or position in which it is to another. All the rest of whatever any creature can do merely comes about according to the laws of nature. The human hand with its opposable thumb is nature's best device for picking up and carrying: man has the best equipment in the world for putting things where he wants them or manipulating them where they lie. The immensely greater portion of the changes he effects in the world, he makes with his hands. Most other creatures which can seize and carry must do so with the mouth; an organ which cannot well be modified for these specific purposes since its primary function of eating is biologically even more exigent. Or they must move things by kicking or shoving with extremities whose main function is transportation of the organism, and whose next most essential use is for self-defense.

Grasping and holding with the hand not only allows more precision of manipulation; it also serves to increase external effects produced with minimal injury to the organism itself. After climbing, and picking and eating, and striking and scratching in self-defense, men probably learned, as the next most profitable use of hands, to pound things with stones, where pounding with the hands themselves or stamping with the feet would be less productive of the desired effect and also threaten injury. Pounding, abrading, grinding, and cutting with selected stones allowed the shaping of things, thus making possible the first artificial implements of human life. It it thus that it became possible eventually for man to produce fire (perhaps allowing him to come down from the trees and live on the ground); to transport himself across waters which he could not swim; to kill at a distance; to move by means of wheels what he could not drag or carry; to harness winds and falling waters for the doing of what is beyond his muscular power; and finally to fly although he has no wings.

However, the multiple possibilities of doing which hands allow could not be exploited without the complexity of brain and of mentality to correspond; just as, conversely, what human mentality makes possible could not be well realized without the skill of hands. The physical possibilities of doing open to other animals are so relatively few, and the situations in which these more restricted modes of physical doing may make a vital difference come so near to being stereotyped, that the government of behavior by automatic or instinctive or conditioned response, without deliberation, is sufficient to secure as adequate adjustment of behavior to environment as the physiological equipment of the organism would in any case allow. It would make no extraordinary difference to other creatures if they should possess some nearer to human mentality: even if they understood more, there would be so little they could do about it, with only teeth, and either claws or hoofs, as their instruments. (I leave it to those of more fertile imagination to set forth the frustrations of Oscar the intelligent coelacanth, or record the tribulations of the boy who dreamed he was a pony.)

For the creature which can manipulate things in that measure which the use of hands makes possible, the environment presents correspondingly more frequent and more complex opportunities for bringing about, and allows of immensely more precise adjustment to an immensely wider range of external circumstances. But in order to take advantage of these wide-ranging possibilities, more complicated and further-reaching modes of mental apprehension are also required. And if we should ask ourselves which counts for more, hands or brains, in the differentiation of humans and their manner of living from other creatures and the kind of life to which they are restricted, then it would seem impossible to answer: it is like asking which is more essential in a watch, the mainspring or the balance-wheel. But it will be in point to observe that it has taken centuries—millennia even—for men to capitalize, so far as they have, upon the possibilities which open out to them by use of their manipulative skill; and that there is no end in sight. Most of what we would account important, in raising the general level of human life by alterations of the environment which we have the physical capacity to effect, has come about since there has ceased to be any significant biological modification of the human hand. It would be likewise true—perhaps in somewhat lesser measure—that the native mental endowment of men has not altered commensurately with this progressive change in human life. It is in the content of our mentality—what we have learned—and not in native capacity, that the correlative and significant change has taken place. And precisely there is a reason why the continuity of the social processes and the social inheritance of ideas must be rated as the decisively essential factors.

But to return to our present point concerning the mental endowment requisite for exploiting the skill of hands: there are three mental characteristics closely related to these potentialities of manipulative skill and the making use of them. First, this multiplication of the possibilities of doing similarly multiplies the alternatives of response which are open, confronting given environmental circumstances, and also increases the degree of specificity with which the effect can be predetermined. Such variety and specificity of possible bringing about do not create the mental capacity consciously to choose and to deliberate our doing, instead of responding automatically to stimulation, but they render that capacity notably and vitally more effective, allowing it to make a kind of difference which will count. Only the creature which can devise things has any great use for foresight, beyond the immediately impending and beyond those repetitive types of situation against which nature can sufficiently provide by built-in modes of response. Only the tool-using animal finds it of much import to plan his action in advance, as against reacting to circumstances as they arise. And only the animal so provided with artificial implements is likely to have more than one life-saving alternative of doing in the presence of danger. Only the creature which can make things and transport them can advantage by any possession beyond some store of food, or find possessions anything but impedimenta, or find a life which is encumbered with them more satisfying to live than one in which there is nothing to do in the morning but get up and go.

Second, only for the creature which can manipulate and devise things is there any necessity for, or notable advantage in, the capacity to imagine —or at least to imagine in self-directed ways as against ungoverned mental association. It has been questioned by some psychologists whether any animal but man has this power of "creative imagination."

And third, it is questionable whether, without such power of governed imagining, there could be any explicit foresight beyond the sensuously conveyed; any apprehension of what is distant in time or space, and hence any content for or possibility of deliberate thinking. The animal may gain his goal object or be thwarted in his instinctive drive, and finally he meets his doom without anticipation; but only human life can be fateful. Only the mind of man can set a continuing aim whose attainment circumstances may permit or disallow; only man can frame a life-purpose, or unite with others in ends which may extend beyond his generation and whose realization must be for him a matter of faith. Only men can set standards or entertain ideals.

Another condition of the possible attainment of the human kind of life—and one frequently mentioned as distinctive of the species—is language. Something akin to language is essential to anything beyond the most primitive forms of group living and warranting application of the adjective "social." All the social animals, including the social insects, have some means of communication. But human speech, over and above its extraordinarily greater complexity, differs from any "animal language" both in the significance of it as communication and in the content which can be communicated. What animal cries express is a feeling aroused in the one who makes them, and what they incite in others of the same species is likewise a feeling; most often a feeling or an urge to do which is similar to what is felt by the individual whose cry is so evoked. The communication is of contagious emotion or contagious urge to response, such as might also be induced by observed behavior of other sorts in members of the group. If animal communication goes beyond the mere calling of attention, the human phenomenon which it resembles most is the spread of excitement in a crowd rather than the imparting of information or the exchange of ideas of those who deliberate together. To what extent the higher animals may recognize the communicative effect of their cries it is beyond my competence to say, but in any case the communication retains the quality of the ejaculative and expressive rather than the assertive or genuinely informational. At most, it is instigative rather than ideational. Human cries of like character retain the same function: there is little in animal mentality which is alien to the human. Man's pre-Neanderthal inheritance is still built-in; presumably what he principally has lost is only the blazing acuity of uncomplicated and undistracted aesthesis. It is also true, of course, that in others of the higher animals short of man, the conditioning of responses begins to be complex. We seem to see in them some muting of merely impulsive reaction, as in the dog who patently crowds down his cringing before a bigger one. On the point in question, we may think to observe in other animals some suppression of the ejaculative cry under conditions in which it would be maladaptive, and some reinforcement of it or inducement of it where it may serve a communicative function.

On this point, as on others, flat contrasts between ourselves and other animals may indeed represent an oversimplification; and it may be well to pause here to observe that general fact. We are but one product of vertebrate and mammalian evolution. But if we here omit the qualifying thoughts so suggested, that will be no serious matter for our present purposes: it is the differentiae which mark the species, and it is the species which we here would understand. It would be equally oversimple to interpret ourselves merely in terms of what we have in common with other creatures. Furthermore, in regard to phenomena whose significance is social, we are at the furthest remove from what is organic to the individual and physiological. If we would trace the eventual product of human civilized living to its roots in the human organism and its functioning, where differences from the animal may judiciously be taken as matters of degree, it will still be appropriate to rate such background and causal factors in terms of the notable contrast between human and animal life for which they are responsible.

In the case of language, the notable difference of the human from the animal is not in organic structure and functioning—though obviously there may be such difference—but in the content of what can be communicated. The expressive language of other creatures is narrowly restricted to what is immediately felt. The mockingbird or the parrot commands a range of sound-production comparable to the human, but what it can so convey to another of its species is no more than what the crow can signalize—its own presence, danger, sex-feeling, available food, and perhaps some others of its own immediate promptings. Even in exceptional cases such as the hive-returning dance of the worker bee, which we interpret as conveying the direction and distance of available nectar, it is questionable whether there is genuine communication of information or merely of surprisingly specific instigative feeling, or automatic adjustment of motor-set, to the specificities of this stimulus.* In general, the range of animal communication is limited to immediate sense and affective feeling, and is as unspecific as these feelings. It is

* If we would summarize the evolutional development which is highly probable—it could hardly be otherwise—we may say that language is first ejaculative and affective; expressive of the mode of feeling. It may thus become evocative or hortatory for the hearer and, as calling attention to, become also and in that sense demonstrative. But this does not yet extend to that sense of the objective which is substantive and which we call in logic "denoting." Demonstration is limited to the here and now. Denoting requires a generality of reference which is not thus limited; requires thinking *of;* and can only come with a kind of reference in which entertainment of the indemonstrable and, so to say, hypothetical is included. Cognition, calling for *representation* and a signifying of the predictive and possible-to-be-experienced, cannot dawn before such entertainment of the absent and the hypothetical. And communication of the cognized and thought of, requires a linguistic vehicle which can convey this mode of hypothetical entertainment.

Since the absent and merely thought of, in contrast to the present and felt, is not automatically or appropriately evocative, the language of cognition is relatively divested of its emotive tone. And correlatively, to govern oneself by reference to the cognitive is to govern oneself deliberately and not emotively. Similarly, the implications for action which are cognitively recognized may be recognized as *imperative,* just because they are *not* automatically moving and emotive. Imperative and emotive, so far from being synonymous, are in fact antithetic.

confined to gross generalities and to the present and actual. The future but not impending, the past but now recalled, the absent but considered, this as compared or contrasted with that, the possible but not actual, and in general the bringing to attention of what is neither observed nor presently observable; all these are quite beyond its possibilities of communication. But without such modes of common thought and the imparting of it, no group could frame a plan or unite on a policy or make an agreement affecting the future and depending on contingencies not presently determined. Only humans can direct attention to the absent, or make commitment with respect to the unobservable or suppositious, and only human speech can convey such modes of thinking. On such points the range of human language, as of human thinking, is as far beyond the animal as the boundaries of the world of which we may be so advised are beyond the horizon of animal vision. And the world of human thought and expression is as multifariously more complex as it is bigger.

The intricate complexities of human cooperation and the corresponding complexities of civilized social organization would be quite impossible without the unlimited variety of the distinguishable series of noises we can emit, or series of marks which we can differentiate and recognize, expressive of the equally complex and intricate thoughts which we can think. It is so that we can direct attention to the unobservable, and convey the merely imagined but perhaps believable, even though it is to be disclosed only in the remote future or contingently upon some complicated train of directed action. That noises made or marks on paper should communicate among us the present state of China, or a future eclipse of the moon, or the structure of a molecule, or can effect agreement to build a house or common agreement to observe a law, is as miraculous as it is commonplace. And the miracle of the human social order is built upon such miracles of human thought and speech. It is so that we can live together in our progressively more complicated civilization and can cooperate to mold the future of it. But we do well to observe how tenuous are these strands upon which our mutuality depends. In that society which is essential to the human kind of life, our most exigent necessities depend upon our common dreams of what is not presented to our senses. The weblike intricacy and delicacy of them is not to be dealt with rudely or approached with blunt instruments.

This gift of language is also and directly essential to the distinctive feature of the history of man in society as progressive. It is largely involved in learning—both in learning of and in learning how—and is otherwise prerequisite to that continuity of human tradition which is the important and unique feature of the human type of social organization and mainly responsible for our social evolution.

The social inheritance of ideas is directly dependent upon the distinctive character of our language as capable of conveying the absent and not presently observable. The essential point here—both with respect to modes of learning and with respect to the preservation of what is learned—is one which is definite and quite clear: by the use of language men can be advised of that which they do not experience, and even of what they never have experienced. By and large, other animals can be advised only of what they might themselves verify at the moment. And because of that, each generation of them must painfully relearn, by its own vicissitudes, all that the preceding generation likewise had to learn; and any learning of an individual by experience peculiar to him will be of profit to no other. The only restriction upon this concerns what can be learned by imitation, or taught as the infant seal is taught to swim. These are, to be sure, important modes of learning, and they persist in humans. They represent that fundamental kind of learning by which what is most exigent for life, but not governed by native instinct, is acquired by the individual of any species. But such learning—be it noted—is confined to learning to do, and learning to do what the preceding generation also did. It does not go beyond what the individual must otherwise acquire by trial and error, and its principal significance is in abbreviation of the learning period and in protection from the hazards of such experimental doing. In other respects, it does not differ from learning by the conditioning of individual experience, and does not markedly extend beyond that.

The contrast here in point is, of course, with that mode of learning which is peculiar to man; learning by being told. For the human, learning by personal experience is learning the hard way. To learn by verbal instruction or by the advisement of presently unobservable fact is an enormous vital economy: an economy in point of time, as well as in the saving from blundersome ineptness in finding out, and an economy in the avoidance of grief and pain. I have been told of an ape who knew that the bananas were behind the closet door and had spent much time in endeavor to get at them. Then, seeing his master grasp the hand-hold of the latch and depress the thumb-piece until it clicked and the door swung open, the ape said "Hoh," and thereafter opened the door without difficulty. If he had been altogether human he would have said: "Why didn't somebody tell me about that? It would have saved me so much bother."

The ape already has the capacity to learn by observation, in contrast to the frog which will snap twenty times at a baited fishhook before he learns to leave it alone. But, without language, he could not, for example, learn how to open a safe which is in another room or even learn by seeing it opened. Through language, the small child can learn about elephants in Africa, the blind can come to know as much as others about the heavenly bodies, and we can discover the microbes of disease and learn what to do about them, though they are beyond our senses.

One vital importance of the social phenomenon of language is the part it plays in education of the young; in preparing them to adjust to the world in the effective human way, profiting by the experience of past generations of men, and fitting them to take their part in the social order. Learning by being told covers the greater part of that schooling which occupies the twentieth-century human for about one fifth of his lifetime. There has come to be so much to be told, in order to capitalize fully upon our social inheritance, for leading the best life of which the individual is capable, and for full adequacy in assumption of a role in civilized society!

Language is even more, and more obviously, essential to that preservation of accumulated learning which is the root factor in the difference between human life and that of other species. It is an utterly indispensable instrument of that continued and progressive human betterment which history reveals. It serves not only for the lengthwise continuity of whatever works for raising the level of life but also for the breadthwise propagation of such learning. Granted real communication, we are warranted in some confidence that there is nothing which is desirable to men at large, and is attainable by any, which will not be eventually shared by all; nor any common trouble which can be obviated by any from which all may not eventually be freed. If communication be maintained, then there could not well be any manner of common human want or ill, so it be curable at all, which must not finally yield before the cumulative weight of socially preserved and socially transmitted learning; especially so, if we remember that learning is not confined to information but includes the knowledge of good and evil.

Finally, we should not fail to recognize that the social conditions for achievement of the good life which lie in the education of the individual and the social inheritance of ideas not only are responsible for the character of human history as progress but—after a certain time at least—continually operate to accelerate the rate of progressive change. What aeons may have elapsed before men fashioned the first tools, we can barely guess; and from that indeterminate date to the dawn of history is a period which still must be measured in terms of geologic ages. What cannot well escape us is that in the few thousand years for which we can tell the story of man in any detail and with any assurance, the conditions and the manner of his living must have altered in larger measure than in all the millennia preceding. And the changes which have come about in the two hundred years since Watt invented the steam engine are, in turn, something like as considerable in effect as all that took place in two thousand years before. Social learning, in being cumulative, also becomes increasingly selective of the more valuable and more effective instrumentalities in the total body of what is learned. Also such ideational factors in the historical process are those which are not expended in being used but are infinitely reusable: ideas, once acquired, are the cheapest of all capital goods, as well as the most productive.

It lies in the nature of the case that the greater the store of learning and the more effective the use which is made of it, the more numerous and the more rapid in rate will be those changes which causally depend upon it. If already the rate of social transformation and the complexities so introduced make us a little dizzy, still it seems quite possible that "we haven't seen anything yet." There could even be a danger that the accelerated pace of that advance which derives from wider information and increased know-how, and the complications of the social organization dictated for the effective exploitation of this kind of learning, may outreach and overwhelm the slower processes of social criticism and social integration. The doubt is whether the forces so let loose may escape from our control and no longer be directed to what is humanly desirable.

There is also question whether the strain of adjustment so put upon our native equipment of intelligence and emotion, and especially upon our mores, may rise to the point where it becomes of itself an outstanding human problem. The individual is still born with the same biological equipment as in the dawn of history. But the life he lives moves further and further away from that to which, by this endowment, he is natively prepared to adjust. Mores and the education of the individual, as themselves functions of society, must bear a continually increasing weight, and impose upon the individual a continually increasing demand for modification of his behavior and redirection of his native impulses. To be a civilized man, prepared to live a civilized life, becomes an ever more complex requirement. And the social necessity to make judicious and humane provision for this adjustment of the individual to the life he now must live, is ever more demanding, and a more complex demand, upon the society itself.

Without a bedrock of social mores, and clarity in social aims, the possibility of further progress could be prejudiced, and the quality of individual life could be sacrificed in some breathless attempt at readjustments too pervasive and too beset by personal frustration for the human framework to endure. Perhaps we near that juncture where it would be opportune to inaugurate a five-year plan for reflection and meditation upon this kind of fact.

Certain it is that the time now approaches when, if even the presently acquired store of information and know-how were to become universally shared and commonly exploited among men, the major remaining problem would hardly be that of further conquest of the natural environment but instead that of human self-control and self-direction.

Once more in history, the understanding which man most needs is self-conscious and self-critical understanding of himself. And this time it is beyond all doubt that the requirement is to understand himself as a social animal, if he wishes to control his further history.

2

THE PRINCIPAL INGREDIENTS

2. THE PRINCIPAL INGREDIENTS

We have so far failed to point out one distinction of the human: man is the self-satisfied animal; he believes in in his own superiority. But if, in some Aesopian fable, the other creatures should gather round him, one may be sure they would dispute this claim. The elephant would deride his puny size. The tiger would challenge him to trial of the issue by mortal combat, divested of his unsporting artificial aids and playing the game according to the universal ground rules. The fox would disparage his poor skill in evasive tactics, and the deer his lack of fleetness. The bear would laugh at his nakedness before the elements, and the tortoise remind him that he has no hard shell for safe retreat. And the condor need only spread his great wings in silent mockery. But man would call their attention to the lesson of history, warning the elephant that if he behave otherwise than as obedient servant his tusks may be made into billiard balls; reminding the bear that man does not need to grow fur in order to use it for protective covering; and observing to the others that if they thwart his will there is danger that the last of their tribe may soon or late be found, stuffed, in a museum. Then, shaking his DDT-can at any insects in the gathering, he can take off to pass the condor at the speed of sound.

On reflection, that ending is not quite right, is it? Let us revise. At the conclusion of this colloquy the owl sums up, admitting that man possesses remarkable instruments in his nimble fingers and his facile wits, and may indeed, by the advantage that these afford, reduce the other creatures to living in his shadow. But he cautions that survival in competition does not prove superiority; it proves only the ability to survive—and we must not commit the naturalistic fallacy.

We ought indeed to thank any owl for reminding us that the real question here is one of worth or value; and no appeal to biological characteristics and capacities or to survival and power to prevail, or even to cosmic history itself, can settle that issue. Concerning everything that is or will be and all that happens, there is this other question whether it is good or bad, and whether it would be better if it were otherwise. We are indeed interested in the question of survival and in what may come to dominate, but the focus of that question is upon the persistence and ascendancy of what is good. Insofar as it should be evil which prevails, it would be bad that this is so. Even confronting the cosmos, we cannot dismiss it as meaningless to ask whether this be a good world or a bad one in which we live. Lest that seem to us a fatuous question, and any answer to it windy metaphysics, let us remark that in any small attempt we make to affect the future—and that is all that any man can do in life—our effort will be empty and irrational without the conviction that the total state of affairs will be infinitesimally better if we succeed.

But how is it, then, that man acquires this conceit of himself, if not by appeal to natural sanction—by this criterion of survival and the power to allocate to himself whatever of the earth's resources meet his needs? Is it merely because he judges by his own anthropomorphic standards, and is thus bound to set himself just below the angels by reason of his parochial manner of assessment? So to adjudge the matter would be jejune—we may easily so come to think the question empty. Man is the only creature that can ask it; and having posed it, he seems to have only these two alternatives; of an answer captured in advance by the terms in which judgment of it will be made, or one by reference to cosmic fact and the sanction supposedly implied by what nature tolerates and seems to foster. Even if this second alternative be chosen, can we expect to do otherwise than set up some *petitio principii*, reading into nature an order of higher and lower by some criterion of characteristics unconsciously chosen because they point to us—our organic complexity, for example, as against the simplicity of the amoeba by which their species seems able to survive indefinitely; or the brain-weight ratio—forgetting about the birds?

The answer is, of course, that we might easily decide that man cannot transcend the limits of what is relative to his human nature and the standards implicit in it, if it were not for the fact that, paradoxically, this conclusion is ruled out because it implies that we can. We could only come to it by standing above the limitations which we so observe and criticizing our human mode of judgment as—so it must be assumed—some superior being would make criticism of it. Those who would so impeach our integrity in assessments of value and correctness, unconsciously presume their own godlike superiority over the rest of us who—they charge—innocently judge within our human limitations. Any self-criticism or self-judgment unavoidably presents this manner of paradox. The self that finds mistake or invalidity inevitably claims superiority over the self that is subject to this error or this fallacy. If we can ask the question *whether* the judgments of worth which we make are merely relative to our subjectivities, then it is already implied that we can determine correctness of an answer to it, and that in such answer we can free ourselves of the subjectivities suspected. Among the superiorities which the self-critical animal inevitably claims for himself is the capacity for just this kind of possible self-transcendence.

The requirement to make assessment of worth and of validity beyond the bounds of what is merely subjective and relative to himself, is one which the self-conscious being cannot set aside. To repudiate it would vitiate his every purpose, consciously and deliberately adopted. That which is aimed at must be better than what already is, and better than what will be without the satisfaction of this aim; otherwise the aim is fatuous and any activity directed to it reduces—as Schopenhauer would have it—to a nauseous inability to quell the striving will. Even this pessimistic and self-negating aim must validate itself by posing its projected end of self-elimination as a better state of things worth attaining. No; the innocent animal that acts on impulse and knows of good and evil only as feelings visited upon him, may escape all question; but the creature that sometimes must decide his act cannot repudiate the question of a good and bad which is not relative to his inclination merely: he cannot fail to judge of worth among the alternatives from which he has to make his choice. He may do better or he may do worse, and knowing the better he may do the worse; but choose he must. And if it occur to him that from some point of view, infinitely removed from his illusionment, there is no better and no worse but thinking makes it so, still he will but commit the completest of all self-frustrations if he decide that it is better not to choose. Where all decisions should be without validity, that decision would be the apotheosis of pointlessness. The self-conscious being, able to deliberate his act and attitude, is stuck with the necessity of doing so: he has no alternative but to choose, and to recognize a better which holds a mandate for his choosing.

If there were nothing more at stake than the question of man's place in the great chain of being, then indeed we might dismiss this matter as of small import. But it is this same kind of question of the assessment of worth which has to be met when we compare one stage of man himself in history with another; and indeed when any fundamental issue of social policy is before us. And it is this kind of question which has to be met when we must settle upon our attitude toward some other social organization which might encroach upon us or be imposed upon us if we fail to be clear and resolute in our convictions of the valuable and valid. If there be no better and worse which is other than merely relative to those who entertain opinion of it, then where shall we find justification of our own projected ends, unless by appeal to force or to some supposition of a cosmic road roller, bound to flatten under it one party or the other in the course of time? Are we by way of quarreling with one another, and sacrificing lives perhaps, in the attempt to bolster our subjective slant on things; or in our avidity to lay a bet on an already determined and inevitable outcome?

We shall not accept such self-stultifying suppositions. If intelligence could be satisfied of the validity of these, then intelligence and the purposes which intelligence sanctions would not be valid to themselves. If men account themselves more fortunate than other creatures in their natural endowment, it will be on the ground that, by the critical and self-critical capacities so vouchsafed to them, they are privileged to achieve a life which is a better life to live. And if they are interested in the direction of any continuing process they discover in the cosmos, that interest will, if serious, find its final point in the quality of conscious life which this cosmos will support and perhaps may foster. With respect to their own history as a species, they may be gratified to find out the facts merely because they are the facts, and facts relating to themselves; but the peculiar point of that interest will still be in the bearing of this process upon what in common men deem good. They will assess this history as one of progress or of retrogression by reference to the common goals of the human will, and the nearer or less near approximation of it to the ends so set.

Even for that relatively trifling question posed by our concocted fable, we can set the criterion of judgment if not prove the application of it. If we account ourselves more privileged than other creatures, it will be on the supposition that, as the time-worn saying has it, it is better to be Socrates dissatisfied than a pig satisfied. And that will be so because Socrates, whatever his dissatisfactions, still finds his life more gratifying to live than that of any pig. And if the pig is satisfied, that will be only because he is unable to imagine what he is missing. Indeed the pig has no primal urges, in the fulfillment of which he may find satisfaction, which are not likewise known to men; and, as John Stuart Mill observed, the judgment of relatively better quality is only to be made by those who are familiar with both terms of the comparison. There have even been men in history whose predicament was remotely similar to that of the pig; as also there still are men whose lives have heretofore been lived outside the main stream of progress and who now discover what they have been missing and are made dissatisfied by that. The present turmoil in the world has some connection with that fact.

Among the peculiar satisfactions reserved to men, and those of which they could least of all endure to be deprived, there is the privilege of seeking and gaining by their own initiative—and, if the gods be kind, of progressively gaining in increasing measure—ends which they have critically assessed and deliberately have chosen as their own. It is in this possibility of progressive approach to whatever stand to them as their self-determined goals that men are free. And in this connection we shall mean by "freedom" not merely that liberty which consists in the absence of compulsion or constraint imposed by others but, more broadly, in the scope of the concrete possibilities open to the individual for *realizing* ends which satisfy his will. In these terms, liberty connotes mainly such independence as the individual has of his community, but the freedom he enjoys will include much which can only accrue to him through the attainments of his social order and by reason of its legacy from the past. It is this freedom progressively to achieve self-chosen goals which is, for men, the highest good of all, and essential to all other goods save only those of sheer good fortune.

That man does indeed possess this privilege of self-determination and self-realization; that he possesses it not merely as an individual and within his individual life, but also possesses it as a race, and by the participation of individuals in the social process; that this social process is unlike that exhibited by any other species; and that, as affecting the generations of men, it represents an evolution which, again, has no parallel in that of any other creature—these are old thoughts which we would here renew. If there is something to be added to them, that may lie in the fact that whereas this view of man and his life in history has sometimes been conceived of as a transcendental mystery, we would present it here as a matter of quite plain fact and as resting on grounds it is not too difficult to make out.

We have already touched upon the factors which underlie this fact. The progressive modification of human life, from the remote beginnings of man to the present day, is distinctively a social evolution. Even for a creature otherwise endowed as man is, nothing like this march from primitive savagery to modern civilization could be conceived of as taking place without the social habit. Particularly it is the progressive raising of the level at which human life is lived which must impress us. There is no correlated biological transformation of the organism to explain it. Also while this evolution may, in many of its aspects, depend upon the natural environment, still such environmental factors must be rated as permissive or limiting, or as contributory rather than instigative of this alteration in the picture of human life, since external nature represents those forces affecting human life which themselves are relatively permanent or change most slowly. It is not so much geologic epochs or geography as it is the migrations of men; not so much the presence or absence of natural resources as man's learned exploitation of them, or exhaustion of them, which have made historic differences. Again, men and other creatures have, at all times and in all places, equally been exposed to the same environing conditions and, that being so, any differential effect of them in the history of man as contrasted with that of other species, cannot be explained except by reference to factors internal to man himself.

It is further true that, though human evolution

is essentially social, the secret of it is not to be found merely in the social habit. Other species share this habit, but their modes of group living alter only as the biological inheritance or some external factor alters: the peculiar human fact is the evolution of society itself, and at a rate which outpaces any change in the environment or any modication of the organism. In the case of the social insects, dependence of group and individual behavior upon biological inheritance would seem to be nearly complete: under changed conditions in which instinctive modes of behavior are insufficiently adaptive, they simply perish. And in other animals which show larger capacity for modification of group habits to meet new conditions, the altered habit will presumably become stabilized as soon as a new equilibrium with environment is established, and thereafter will persist unchanged. Only human modes of life evolve while both biological inheritance and environing conditions remain substantially the same.

There is a sense in which this evolution is independent even of the inherited psychological capacities and tendencies of the human individual. For example, the intelligence-quotient of Athenians in the Age of Pericles could not have been much different from our own; but the products of intelligence, in our more extensive understanding and control of nature and in the structure of our living supported by technology, is vastly changed. Nor should we suppose our native equipment of emotion and inclination to be much altered; but the institutions governing our social activities and our communal relationships are different and notably more complex.

Some form of group living comes near to being a biological necessity for the human animal; man's long infancy, if nothing else, would dictate the continuing family group at least. And as with other social animals, his social bent is presumably native and represents a primal urge. But the social order which eventually comes to characterize the human represents no biological necessity—even if it has a biological sanction—nor any unmodified gregarious instinct. In the complex interrelations of individuals which our modern social order dictates, it far outruns any psychological bent of association and may, as we suggested earlier, go to that point where the required social adjustments become a frequent and serious kind of psychological problem for the individual. Indeed the disparity between our native inclinations and social requirements accounts for one outstanding type of social phenomena—all those connoted by "social control." We do not, like the bees, behave amenably to social needs because we have no counter inclinations. Even the need of individual *self*-control arises, in good measure, from native antisocial urges. On this point, human society and insect societies are antithetic rather than comparable, and the evolution of the human social order is, in measure, a triumph over rather than a dictate of our native human feelings. On the part of the individual—and this is a crucial point—it bespeaks the control of primal emotive urges and natural inclinations by intelligent understanding of what individual well-being and welfare of the organized group require. It is significant of mores and the essential self-constraint of the moral. As intelligent, it calls for the capacity to submit the solicitations of the here and now sensed and felt to the control of the future and of what is otherwise remote and represented merely and has no impact on us at the moment. And as rational and moral, it calls for that self-criticism and self-restraint which is implied in weighing one's own behavior as a manner of behavior likewise open to other members of the group, and as compatible with the maintenance of group living and the effectiveness of it in the attainment of common interests.

Both intelligence and rational self-discipline in action are, of course, more widely significant than in the bearing of them upon group living and the social organization. Also, as men have always known, individual capacity and attainment in both these respects always falls short of the ideal, and the exercise of it is subject to lapses. Still so much of these capacities as is possessed and exercised stands as *sine qua non* for all the difference of human from animal living, and is basic for the mode of sociality which is peculiar to the human, and for that evolution of the social organization which is confined to man.

Human living and the habits of men alter progressively because the human inheritance alters progressively. But this progressively enriched inheritance is not biological, and it is environmental and material only so far as the material environment is a product of it and not its cause. It is a legacy of socially acquired ideas and customs of behavior, and the social order is itself the transmitting agent. We are born without knowledge or understanding. Our native response-mechanisms are even less well adapted for survival than is the case with other animals; and our biological endowment of feeling and emotion is little different from that of men in the Old Stone Age. Society, however, intervenes at birth and promptly begins the molding of the individual into its own image; first ministering to his physical needs for survival and development and then beginning the transformation of him into a civilized being by that long and complex process which is the education of the individual. Here the relative lack of ready-prepared and instinctive adaptation in the human infant has even a kind of left-handed biological sanction: given the fact that, within society, such helplessness is not itself too maladaptive, it has the advantage that with some blunting of the acuity of native impulses there is less of the primitive endowment to be unlearned. A nearer to blank tablet more readily takes the impress to be socially imposed and offers less impediment to social training.

Beyond the conditioning of responses, in which the learning of the human is like that of any other species, the two broad aspects of education are the imparting of information and the inculcation of mores; and the neglect of either of these—as it will do no harm to remind ourselves—is to the peril of the individual and to any society in which he is to find a place. And as we should also remind ourselves, the education of the human animal never ceases but, as learning from the social give-and-take, persists throughout his lifetime. It is only by this education of individuals, generation after generation, that they come to share in the cumulative social inheritance, and it is only so that the heritage of ideas is preserved and passed on. Without this extensive education man would probably be little different from the apes, and human life little different from that of the anthropoids in general.

It lies in the nature of the case that the first acquired treasures of this social inheritance will represent such learning as will serve for meeting the most exigent human needs. And these are principally two; first, such mores as are essential to preservation of the group and maintaining group life, and second, that kind of learning required for provision of the material necessities of life. These two represent the minimum requirements for human survival. And they likewise represent two grand divisions of the human tradition and of social institutions; on the one side, the moral-political-legal, and on the other, the scientific-economic-technological.

The power of the cumulative social inheritance, and what heights it can eventually reach in improvement of the quality of life, has no more convincing exemplar than in the field of the technological and economic. To observe this fact, be it noted, is not to set these as the highest in the scale of human values but only to recognize them as most exigent. Also the evidence of attainment is here more easily impressive both because what is achieved relates to unqualifiedly universal needs and because the evidence of attainment, being material and tangible, is such that he who runs may read. It is a paradox even, and one with respect to which many have been misled, that although the goods to which technological and economic activities are directed are for the most part vested in the material, and the needs they satisfy are among those which are primary and primitive, the causal factor in the progressively better fulfillment of them is the immaterial one of accumulated learning and the social tradition which transmits it, along with other constituents in the cultural idea-system. The *economy* in economics, and the correlative multiplication of material goods, is *exclusively* accounted for by acquired and socially transmitted know-how. In "labor power" there has been no advance whatever in human history, unless in the sense that the population has increased. The improvement of life with respect to material needs is *totally* due to the progressive utilization of ideas, in displacement of the expenditure of muscular energy, as the causal factor in production. If social justice called for the delivery of the full value of goods produced to those responsible for the production of them, then the greater part of our economic wealth must be delivered to our ancestors for the labor-saving techniques they have bequeathed to us.

We intend here no observation concerning the important problems of economic justice, beyond pointing out the absurdity of any attempted solution of them based on a causal theory of economic value. The point is that identification of economic forces with the material is an extraordinary oversight of the plainest facts. If any civilized group of men should be shorn of all their material inheritance from past generations and even of all they had themselves produced, but should still retain their inheritance of technological and economic know-how, their loss could still be made good in something like a generation. But if, by some unimaginable cataclysm, they should be left with all their accumulated material wealth and artifacts intact, but wholly bereft of all that man has learned in history and of their personal recollections of the same kind, then as soon as their store of consumable goods should be exhausted—which must be soon—they must begin over again at the level of ape living, and perhaps take a stretch of time comparable to that since men themselves lived like apes, in order to regain their present patrimony.

Since material goods include the necessities of life, the economic needs—along with the equally exigent need for safety and hence for the preservation of the group—must be dominant until these requirements are satisfied in fair measure. But let us reflect upon the sober and clear fact already mentioned that if it were not for human stupidities on other points and for the impediments to effective communication and our learning from one another, men might find themselves already at that point where the reasonable exploitation of technological and economic knowledge could assure a high level of life for all mankind—so far as that level is to be measured in terms of meeting material needs—and perhaps with no greater expenditure of human energy than is conducive to physical and mental health. The supposition that, beyond that point, the economic categories must still be dominant in our culture, implies a highly depressing conception of human intelligence, and suggests that the human animal already approaches that equilibrium with the natural environment beyond which there will be no road but back.

The economic category of social phenomena also exemplifies other implications of the dominance in human history of the inheritance of ideas. The cumulative store of useful learning, both as acquired information and as acquired know-how, must at some point outrun the capacity of any individual to command it all. And once that point is passed, both the exploitation and the transmission of learning become further possible only by the division of learning and of vocations, and the specialization of social functions. The complex aspects of the social order which depend on that are by no means confined to those whose significance is economic; and it may be regrettable to omit notice of similar facts in other categories of the social. But as before, the economic illustrations are perhaps the most easily observed. Specialized skill reaches a higher pitch, and specialized learning a deeper penetration. The immense effects of such division and specialization of social functions in the maximizing of effective accomplishment and the minimization of effort would be difficult to exaggerate. It will need no emphasizing: the evidence today is all about us. Nor will it be necessary to dwell upon such further consequences as the continually increasing complexity of the social organization, and the consequent strain so put upon morals and mores to keep up with the progressively expanding problems of social control and direction of the over-all social purposes. What may be of nearly equal importance to the increase of material wealth, in raising the general level of life, and might more easily escape due notice, is the effect of it in increasing exploitation of individual aptitudes and allowing more freedom of choice in the development and exercise of them. Particular aptitude and special skill are normally accompanied by satisfaction in the exercise of them. Men enjoy most what they do especially well; both because it represents their most facile accomplishment and because superior attainment ministers to their self-respect and sense of status. Specialization of social functions not only contributes to higher effectiveness but it minimizes those erosions of the spirit which are not altogether eliminable in any type of human endeavor and enhances the possible satisfactions of achievement. It likewise allows, in larger measure, that peculiar social satisfaction which may be found in contributing, at one and the same time, to private welfare and to the common good. At the best, this specialization of function can approximate to the ideal of making our own living by doing that which, if we had no necessity to secure a livelihood, we should most like to do in life. That is perhaps the greatest boon which a society could secure to an individual. And that this ideal should be approachable by many, perhaps should stand as the highest mark of a good society and one of the finest fruits of any social heritage.

Incidentally we may observe that this ideal of life in the economic aspect of it is most nearly approachable in those specializations called professional. It is in such vocations that the exercise of aptitude and acquired skill is most free, as it is also in them that the possibility of contributing to the life of others, and to the continuing and cumulative social heritage, is plainest. I cannot forbear to mention the privilege of the physician to minister to us in our direst need, and of the teacher, allowed to impart what he can offer to the generation which will surpass him. It is also worthy of an underscore that with the advance of technology there is a correlative advance of economic vocations, a similar multiplication and diversification of them, and a correlative increased measure in which the effective practice of them calls for acquired understanding rather than merely the acquired skill of hands. And one result of this is the multiplication of those vocations which, whether called professions or not, share in measure that prized freedom which marks professional practice.

If it is in technology and the economic that we may see most clearly and be impressed by the power of the social inheritance of ideas for human betterment, it is in science that we may observe most readily and directly the cumulative character of it and the modes of its transmission. Science, at one and the same time, supports and broadens and advances our technological command and gratifies our unlimited curiosity about the world we live in. Science, as we most commonly think of it and as the term is most commonly used today, does not indeed extend to the most important mode of knowledge—the knowledge of human values. Science, in this current and restricted sense, deals only with the means of life; with the instrumentalities available for whatever purposes we may choose to use them; and includes no judgment upon the desirability or the validity of the ends we aim at. But by this confinement to the tangible and the outwardly observable, it likewise restricts itself to what is provable to any man capable of understanding it and endowed with normal sense perception. In science, disagreements are always possible to obviate by adequate experience and investigation. And because it thus concerns that community of knowledge which comes as near as possible to demonstrable certainty, it presents most unmistakably certain essential features of the social inheritance of ideas and its advance. In technology and the economic we observe the fruits of this; in science we may look upon one face of the thing itself.

Here we may see that manner in which, in the cumulative result of the social process of learning, the cognitive capacity of the individual is transcended. Though there can be no scientific finding which is not first the discovery of some individual, and though no lone individual, nor any generation which should not build upon the past, could advance beyond primitive myth in understanding of the world about us, still, as the story of science will suggest, we may be justified in thinking that there can be no secret of nature which is beyond the human capacity eventually to find out. The process of this advance is writ large in history. There is hardly any problem of finding-out on which the first guesses have not been wrong. But the wrong answers have been put to the test and corrected or eliminated. Even when wrong they have stimulated investigation leading to their own amendment. The record has been preserved. There has been continual sorting and sifting and selection, progressive discarding of whatever has proved incorrect, and progressive consolidation and systematization of what has proved correct. And through the continuity of the scientific tradition, any item of scientific truth, once disclosed, becomes a permanent possession of mankind, available to any human aim which it may serve. The truth is socially contagious, even though we may fail to catch it on first exposure; and eventually it must become endemic. Error also is infectious, but through the social process of repeated common deliberation on moot points, we eventually become immune to almost any specific and recurrent error. And what science thus most clearly exemplifies is not confined to the science which so illustrates it.

If we look upon this picture in the large, observing the concrete and undeniable ways in which man moves forward in history, and almost any purpose common to men may be increasingly better met as time goes on, it would seem that there are two things which could hardly fail to impress us. We must be convinced that, in all that is important, the distinctive character of man hardly shows itself in the biological capacities of the individual physical organism, even though there must be root elements in his physical endowment which allow of this distinctive character of the species. The positive force which operates to give him his peculiar power and determine his destiny lies in his capacity to create and maintain a social order which preserves and transmits the conquests of the human mind, and by so doing progressively enlarges and secures to men the possible realization of their common aims.

That history presents no undeviating line, nor indeed any single and unbroken line, and that what we would elicit here is no more than one abstractable aspect; this should go without saying. Nothing would be further from our intention here than to offer a "theory of history." But the march of men toward those goals which they unite upon is no romantic dream; it is the most concrete and best substantiated large-scale fact which history has to record, and prehistory to corroborate. The cumulative power of intelligence, operative through a social order which retains the fruits of past discovery and understanding, and utilizes these for the solution of remaining problems and the attainment of further purposes; this is the peculiar genius of mankind. It is no power resident in the individual as such: he participates and he may contribute. But in what it has created and what may further be achieved, it is as far beyond what the lone individual could stretch to as the time through which it operates is beyond his recollecting or anticipation.

We shall also be impressed with the thought that it is in the continued working of this social transmission of learning and the cumulative inheritance of ideas that our surest hope for the future lies. Indeed we might not be egregious if we suppose that these forces will prove near to irresistible, and certain in the general character of their consequences. There is one interest which is common to all mankind—interest in the improvement of human life. Given some measure of intelligence, given the heritage of the ideas which we possess already and the clear hope of further such conquests, given the social order which will save and transmit these, given the social economy to exploit natural resources, given the instruments of science by which already we can make molecules to our liking and split the atom or harness the sun's heat to add to our supply of mechanical energy almost at will, given the wonder drugs and the techniques of immunization to turn aside contagious diseases and perhaps conquer those which are organic; given all of these resources, is there anything which could dim the hope for the future of mankind—unless some wholly improbable cataclysm of nature or some incredible irrationality on the part of man himself? Yes, there is perhaps just one possibility of disaster still remaining—some extraordinary immoralism combined with great power in the hands of those who thus lack the moral constraints. If history is to be turned back, moral failure will be the explanation. There is nothing else, from now on, which is of such deadly importance for the future of man as a sufficient rationality and a sufficiently developed and effective moral sense.

3

THE CRITICAL FACTORS

3. THE CRITICAL FACTORS

THERE is nothing which is distinctive of the human mentality nor any significant phenomenon of the social organization which is not implicated with the fact of man's capacity for self-direction and self-government. The acquired modes in which the individual learns to direct his doing to projected ends, and his developed convictions of right and wrong in such government of his activities, represent his morals. And the similar learning and convictions of the social group constitute its mores. If there be any over-all direction to be observed in history, and if that direction answers in any measure to a community of human aims and efforts, then it could hardly fail to be the case that this progressive movement, dependent on the confluence of human purposes, must finally reflect some community of moral sense.

Using "moral" in this widest and most important meaning of the word, connoting not merely rightness in our acts toward others but right government of deliberate activities in general, the moral factors are the critical factors of human life altogether. It is these which represent the last arbitrament; the final determination of our purposes and our decisions. They are critical in a double sense; first, that insofar as men have control over the manner of their living and exercise it in ways of which they will themselves approve, the moral factors fix the goals toward which human life is directed; and second, that morals and mores are themselves products of critical reflection and assessment.

There are two main forms of such critical judgment; appraisals of the good and bad, and assessments of the right and wrong. As between these two, it is the sense of good and bad which must be antecedent, and the sense of right and wrong which presumes that and is built upon it. If there should be nothing which greets us in experience with the qualities of good or bad, then plainly there would also be nothing which we should account as right or wrong. The rightness or wrongness of deliberate doing must—either simply and directly or in some manner which is indirect—turn upon some goodness or badness which is at stake in the decision of it. However, the mere encounter with the good and bad in the experience of life is insufficient in itself to lead to any sense of right and wrong. That cannot dawn until behavior becomes responsive not merely to *felt* good and ill, but to a *knowledge* of good and evil; to some understanding of what leads to what in the processes of nature, some insight as to where good and bad are to be found, and some comprehension of those acts within our choosing which will conduce to achievement of the desirable and avoidance of the undesirable. If, as we commonly suppose, men are the only animals capable of such objective knowledge, and capable also of directing their doing by reference to what they know instead of what they feel, then also they must be the only creatures with a developed sense of right and wrong.

The sense of good and bad, by contrast, is primordial to conscious life at large. Indeed it would be plausible that mere feeling of euphoria or dysphoria is the most ancient form of consciousness. Though what is humanly experienced with these qualities has become complex, as the human mentality in general has become complex, still the distinction itself remains basically the same; and the sense of good and bad is something which man brings forward from his prehuman ancestry. Whether by intelligence and deliberate choosing or merely by instinct and ungoverned impulse, all conscious life and action answers to this distinction of the good or bad. Whatever the further characteristics of animal behavior, it still stands as a broadly valid generalization that activity affected by a consciousness tends to the fulfillment of felt need and to the satisfying, and tends to the avoidance of discomfort and distress. Also and in similar broad terms, so far as any creature can be said to learn at all, it tends to repeat those actions which assuage felt drives and to avoid repetition of those which end in frustration or suffering. Consciousness at large turns toward the good, and to the bad it literally is averse. Whether or not this should be a matter of importance to us in any further connection, let us pause to observe that this broad general fact represents a kind of inbuilt teleology correlative with the functioning of consciousness in vital processes.

We might think to explain this correlation between the modes of behavior which are acquired and reinforced and some euphoric quality of the experience to which they lead, by the fact of natural selection: any creature which found it gratifying to do what is maladaptive would tend to be eliminated in consequence of that abnormality. And, resultant from that fact, surviving generations are destined to consist, in progressively larger proportion, of individuals whose natural feelings prompt them to behave in adaptive ways. But let us note that this commonplace depends upon another: it assumes that associated felt satisfaction will prompt to the doing of an act, and that associated pain or frustration will prompt to avoidance of the act which brought it on. That is, of course, the general fact here noted. But we can at least imagine a world in which it should be otherwise; a world in which conscious beings generally should be so constituted that felt pain automatically induced them to persevere in the act which caused it and to repeat this mode of action on later like occasions, and felt satisfaction operated to inhibit action which led to it and induced avoidance of any repetition. In such a world, the conditions of survival and the law that like breeds like would render life progressively less satisfying and more grievous for creatures which survived. Nor is there anything fantastic in this supposition except our comfortable assurance that the actual world is not like that but is the opposite of it.

Let us also note that this relation between desirable qualities of experience on the one side and tendencies of physiological behavior on the other is a *correlation* and, as just observed, one which conceivably could be otherwise. To reduce it to an identity by *defining* the intrinsically good in terms of correlated behavior is an obvious fallacy.* The *purpose* in "purposive behavior," for example, is a phenomenon of consciousness and represents the instigation of behavior by reference to an envisaged end. To define "purposive behavior" in terms of physiological characteristics common to goal-seek-

* To avoid misunderstanding, let us remark that this fallacy, committed by such naturalistic ethical theories as that of Herbert Spencer—who defines good conduct as relatively evolved conduct—lies in confusing factual correlation, or identity of the denotation of terms, with that equivalence of meaning which is the defining relation. This is *not*, apparently, what G. E. Moore would designate as "the naturalistic fallacy," though he charges those conceptions which commit the fallacy described above with "the naturalistic fallacy." Let us also record the conviction that neither the fallacy we here point out nor any which Mr. Moore describes is peculiar to naturalistic theories of ethics or characteristic of all theories of that class.

ing behavior in general, may be a harmless or even propitious methodological procedure in psychology, just as defining the dimensions of heard sound in terms of the correlative dimensions of harmonic motion may be a harmless procedure in physics. It is the business of natural science to establish such correlations, including those universal correlations called laws of nature. But if in fact such correlations represented equivalences of *meaning*, there would be no occasion to call upon science to find them out; they could be determined merely by cogent reflection upon what we supposed ourselves to be talking about. Value terms have their essential significance, finally, by reference to the qualities of consciousness. And to identify what they intend in terms of physical correlates, thus reducing the qualities of conscious life to the status of epiphenomena, is merely to revive old-fashioned materialism in a more sophisticated guise. It rules out, as if negligible, that which, for any understanding of the normative, is head and front of the whole matter.

To seek the good and to avoid the bad is the basic bent of conscious life. And the laws of learning are laws of ameliorating the quality of living by conserving and adhering to what is good, discarding and avoiding what is bad. When as with ourselves, learning becomes in part a self-directed activity, and the results of action come to be consciously assessed as desirable or undesirable, conducement to the good and avoidance of the bad still remains as the rational criterion of such learning and doing as has any rationale. Human understanding vastly increases the range of that to which good and bad apply, by its penetration of the causal processes of nature and its foresight of the remoter consequences of our action. It thus accounts desirable not merely what directly satisfies in the presence of it but whatever is instrumental to the production and possession of such gratifying things. And it rates as bad not merely the directly painful or repugnant but whatever may bring about these things to which we are averse. Also human self-consciousness vastly extends the scope, and complicates and refines the modes, of behavior which is understood as thus leading to some consequence which will prove desirable or undesirable. It is not, however, in any altered attitude toward good and bad as such, but in this comprehension of the relationship between what we do or may do and good or bad results, and in the consequent deliberation of action and self-criticism in doing, that we find what is distinctively human in our apprehension and assessment of values. And it is in such deliberation and deliberate action, self-consciously determined by recognized relation to the good and bad, that we have the human sense of right and wrong.

The root of this sense of right and wrong is, thus, our human knowledge of good and ill in the consequences of what we do. It does not lie in any separate moral faculty or authoritative intuition; instead it is already implicated in those same capacities which distinguish human knowing and thinking from animal apprehension; and in the deliberate government of behavior in the light of recognized objective fact, instead of automatic response to felt stimulus or emotive urge. Instead of learning merely through the modification of his felt impulses as an effect of his past experience, the human animal may learn to direct his action by the cognitive tracing out of causal relationships, and assure the desirability of his doing by inductive generalizations, in trains of thought whose cogency he is capable of criticizing and assessing.

In his possible self-government man is two steps beyond what even the highest of the other animals can attain. The first is his capacity to determine his behavior, not by feeling and the immediate quality of it, but in the light of his cognitive apprehension of the future, the absent, and the possible. He does not have to *feel* the desirability of a more or less remote objective of possible action, by being aroused to vivid emotive response in his envisagement of it, in order to recognize that it *is* in fact desirable. And the second is his ability, by cognitive deliberation upon the past—whether his own experienced past or that of others reported to him—to arrive at a settled judgment of what it is best to do. He is able to adopt an active and criticized attitude toward some whole class of like occasions and even to formulate a general decision for his future conduct; "Under circumstances such and such, do so and so." His deliberated and deliberate actions thus come to be governable in accord with settled convictions, and answerable to maxims, rules, and principles which recommend themselves to his critical reflection. These are, in the large sense, his moral precepts—his directives in self-government of his deliberate doing. And, as we shall see shortly, the sense of right doing as imperative is implicitly contained in that.

The first of these two abilities mentioned—cognitive apprehension of the future, the absent, and the possible, including cognitive appraisal of what is so envisaged as desirable or undesirable—is intelligence. And the second—the capacity to arrive at general convictions, deliberately adopted attitudes, and precepts of conduct, and to guide action by what they sanction—is rationality or reasonableness.

It is doubtful that what is connoted by these two words, "intelligence" and "rationality," represent distinct features of the human mentality. At least they hardly could exist apart. We can perhaps imagine intelligent apprehension of absent and possible goods and bads along with total insouciance toward them: the Cyrenaics recommended that attitude. But the only vital function which intelligence could exercise is that of modifying what we do. Without that office of it, it would effect no difference in the world we inhabit or in the conditions and vicissitudes of our living. Without that pragmatic significance of intelligence, it would have no biological sanction, and it is implausible that evolution would produce or perpetuate a characteristic so ineffectual. One who should thus possess intelligence but fail to modify his action by the advisement of it would be no better off for having this capacity: indeed he might be worse off, being able to suffer his future woes—which he does nothing to avert—in prospect as well as in the visitation of them.

However, in spite of the fact that what we call intelligence and what we call rationality could hardly exist the one without the other, we use these two words to apply to different aspects of our self-government. The explanation of that would seem to lie in the fact that there are two different ways in which we may come to choose the worse instead of the better course of conduct. We may fail to grasp the situation fronted as well as we might; and that kind of failure is "unintelligent," "stupid." Or we may know the better but deliberately do the worse; and that kind of failure in self-direction is "irrational," "perverse."*

In any case, both these native capabilities are essential to any sense of right and wrong. The capacity to act deliberately differs from that unconsidered and impulsive behavior which is common to men and other animals by requiring some measure of explicit foresight of the value-conse-

* The distinction becomes a little clouded in the case in which we must rouse ourselves in order to exercise the best intelligence of which we are capable, and fail to do so. However, if that kind of failure is regarded as an imputable fault, we are also likely to consider it a failure to behave *reasonably*.

quences of the contemplated doing. Beyond that, however, it also requires the capacity to respond to stimuli, not according to the pleasant or unpleasant affective tone of them and the intensity of it, or the gratification of giving rein to the impulse they arouse, but according to the *anticipated* satisfaction of the foreseen *results* of action. It is at this point that the dictate to govern conduct by reference to what we know, instead of the way we feel, takes on the significance of an imperative. We are all more or less stupid, and the failure of foresight—of intelligence—may not be imputed as a fault. But even where there is such foresight, and the capacity to act conformably to it is natively possessed, accord of conduct with the advisement of it is not natively *automatic:* children are not so bent, and even adults often have to be a little stern with themselves about it. It is, thus, "unreasonableness" or "irrationality" which is the directly imputable fault; and the sense of the imperative attaches to the dictate to *conform* to what intelligence advises rather than the dictate *to be* intelligent.

The sense of the imperative characteristically affects those situations in which the course of conduct to which we are advised by foresight of desirable or undesirable results runs counter to the promptings of immediate feeling and inclination —though in a broader sense we speak of any act so sanctioned as imperative regardless of inclination. There is, let us say, some present inclination to do, aroused by solicitations of sense or emotive feeling. But this is accompanied by anticipations of remoter consequences which are expected to be dissatisfying, and dissatisfying to such degree that if they were to be visited upon us immediately, at this moment of decision, their unpleasantness would cancel out any gratification felt in the doing. Premonitions of the unpleasant are unpleasant feelings, but commonly they are not so strongly unpleasant as the unpleasantness anticipated. Thus though these premonitions color the affective tone of the inclination to do, they do not color it so deeply as to transform it into a felt disinclination or revulsion; there would still be satisfaction felt in performing the act and letting the future take care of itself. Or consider the opposite kind of case: an act which we feel disinclined to do is recognized as necessary if some remoter evil is to be escaped. The premonition of later distress may arouse a feeling of urgency, but merely as present feeling it is less intense than the immediate aversion to the act which it would dictate. In either kind of case, the government of action according to the weight of future satisfaction or dissatisfaction as cognitively understood, and not according to the weight of present affective feeling toward it, is the rational way to behave. In such situations, the rational decision is characteristically qualified by a sense of constraint and of the imperative—in the kind of cases cited, of the prudentially imperative. Any attitude or general way of meeting such situations which is sanctioned by this imperative is recognized as prudentially right. And a maxim which formulates such a sanctioned way of acting—"Do not sacrifice your future good to any lesser present good"—is recognized as a valid prudential precept.*

Prudence belongs under the head of morals in that broad meaning of "moral" in which it connotes self-government at large. The prudential sense is, so to say, the beginning of moral wisdom. And the moral sense in the narrower and more frequent meaning of "moral"—restricted to our acts as affecting others—rests upon this wider one. Without the constraint to respect our own interests of tomorrow—not immediate to us now—there could be no psychological basis for extending re-

* More accurately; "So act as to maximize your total probable realizations of satisfaction over time."

spect to the future interests of other persons, which never will become immediate to us and are appreciated only through empathetic imagination, just as our own future experience is presently imagined.

Psychologically, the stretch from prudence to social morals may be a long one; and certainly other factors than this one of an antecedent prudential sense must be involved. We make no pretense here of tracing out the psychological development. But in terms of what must eventually be reached, and looking to the validities involved, the gist of the matter may be briefly put. Given the basic capacity to subordinate immediate feeling to the dictates of the cognitive recognition of objective actualities, and given the intelligence to appreciate the gratifications and griefs of others as realities fully comparable to our own, the imperative to respect the interests of others as we would call upon others to respect our own, is a dictate of rationality.* Recognition of this imperative requires

* We may not account it a failure of rationality if a person puts his own interest first—prudence also is a rational concern. But if it be pointed out to him that his contemplated act will not conform to what he would call upon any other man in his situation to do, and he does not recognize that consideration as constituting a claim upon his conduct, then we *shall* account him irrational.

only that capacity to generalize which is essential to human thinking altogether and is required for any learning to govern our behavior by reference to our representational apprehension of objective facts. More clearly and obviously; a way of acting, to be right in a given case, must be one which would, in the same premises of action, be right in every instance and right for anybody.

Recognition of that basic principle of all social morals is as old and as universal as critical self-consciousness itself and the capacity for articulate formulation of the general. In various forms it is familiar: "Do unto others as ye would that they should do unto you"; "So act that you could will the maxim of your conduct to become a universal law"; "Do no act which contravenes any principle which you would call upon other men universally to respect." If this overarching principle anywhere fails of acknowledgment, that should merely remind us that human perversity is as perennial as the rationality it belies. The consequences of that fact would be even more serious than they are, if it were not that rationality makes for unanimity whereas perversities are various and likely to cancel one another. And if moral perversity is more frequent than perverse repudiation of other rational insights, and history more frequently shows recurrence of moral barbarism than of other forms of stupidity and obliquity, that too has its explanation. Moral enlightenment meets a resistance which other forms of learning do not: we inherit savage propensities of behavior which call for our restraint, as likewise we inherit inclination to the imprudent; but we are born innocent of beliefs. Criticism is always harder to take than information, even when it is self-criticism.

It is also essential to remark that if intelligence and rationality belong to our native endowment, that is in the sense of inborn capacities, and in the further sense that we find it impossible to repudiate their claim upon us, but not in the sense of ready-made and impelling modes of response. The exercise of intelligence and rationality may indeed operate, like any other form of training, so as to approach to habitual conformity. But such exercise can never become automatic in the sense that the optimum which we are so constrained to approach ever ceases to lay further claim upon us and call for further attention and self-discipline.

Among other consequences of these commonplaces, there is the fact that moral and other rational insights, like other forms of learning, call for, and benefit from, social reinforcement. Even the logical sense, which most obviously is attributable to rationality, needs cultivation and benefits from training—though if it were not rooted in the native endowment any inculcation of it would be impossible. Even prudence, which is in some sense the minimal form of moral wisdom, needs inculcation in childhood. In these matters which stand over and above information of existential fact, the last judgment, for any individual, must be his own, and he neither need nor can displace it by that of any other. But that fact does not diminish either the effectiveness or the desirability of the social criticism. All processes of deliberation in the individual mind are speeded up, and frequently corrected, by finding their place in social deliberation. We more quickly arrive at right conclusions, and are surer of them when reached, when we think in company or bring our thinking to the forum. And the significance of "thinking in company" is not confined to vis-à-vis discussion but extends as widely as effective communication on any common problem. Two heads are better than one—and this not merely because two heads may contain more information. Beyond that, it reflects the obverse of a fact already noted: unanimity is a fair index of correctness, since errors are likely to be various. There is the same need to submit moral findings of the individual to the social consensus that there is to check our logical conclusions and our mathematical demonstrations, whose correctness likewise is a matter which does not turn upon empirical information.

The significance of moral learning, and hence of the social process with respect to it, is not, however, confined to such considerations as those just cited. Any principle which could be basic for morals must be highly general and abstract. But that to which it must finally be applied will be some concrete situation in which deliberate decision is called for; an act to be determined under particular conditions which will affect what follows from it and—in the peculiarly moral type of situation—will involve others than the doer in the effects of it. There could be no assessment of a particular act, or of a specific way of acting, as satisfying or failing to satisfy any such basic principle as we have cited without collateral judgment of the consequences of the act, and of these consequences as affecting others for good or ill. And the good or bad consequences of particular ways of acting are something we can learn only from experience. Indeed the reason why fundamental moral principles can be determined as valid without appeal to particular empirical facts is precisely because they become applicable to concrete cases only mediately and through a second premise of another sort. They merely formulate the ultimate *criteria* of morally right action and are definitive of justice. But whether a specific act under particular circumstances will or will not satisfy the criteria they set, they do not and cannot say. They leave that to be determined by the facts of the case—facts about good and bad results of specific ways of acting.

Because of this character of them, principles such as those we have mentioned have sometimes been charged with being "empty"—but only by those who short-sightedly overlook the necessities of the matter and, theoretically, would "cry for the moon": they want, as the basis for ethics, a principle which shall be, at one and the same time, comprehensive enough to extend to every case of deliberate action, but independent of any kind of empirical facts, and yet determine, in every instance, whether the act in question is right or wrong. That is not possible; indeed it involves a contradiction in terms.

What a principle *can* do is, as suggested, to set

the criteria for the judgment of particular cases. And the overarching principle indicated above is, in any of its formulations, sufficient for that.* But it is thus sufficient, as should be noted, only by what is implicit in phrases which refer to "*you*"; what you could will, what you would have others do. And to interpret the principle on this point, it must be observed that such reference is not meant to be personal. It is not intended to suggest, for example, that if you choose to make your daily breakfast of oatmeal and would be content with that as universal practice, you are thereby justified in imposing it on the family. The significance of this "you" is in fact that it directs us to imagine ourselves as *suffering* the act in question and so come to appreciate the consequences of it as good or bad.

On careful examination it will be found that this categorical principle of morals sets two criteria of right action; one formal and explicit, the other contentual and implicit. The formal requirement is

* I take it that the Golden Rule and Kant's Categorical Imperative and the third formulation mentioned above all have the same intent, and that any divergence of them would be too fine a point to affect the general considerations which are most important concerning any one of them.

that of universality and impersonality: whatever is a right way of acting is right in all instances; right for anybody to adopt, in the same premises of action. And that is merely the formal requirement of *being a valid rule,* whether it be a rule of moral action or of logical inferring or of prudential or technical practice. The second and contentual criterion is what is implicit in the reference to what *we could be satisfied with* as a universally prevailing practice. And as a little reflection will make clear, the sense of that matter lies in two things; first, that acts are to be judged according to their good or bad consequences; and second, that such goodness or badness of their effects is to be assessed from the point of view of those upon whom these effects are visited (and from the point of view of the doer only as he is so included).

The formal and ultimate principle is, thus, such as may appropriately be attributed to our rationality; to our capacity to recognize valid precepts which are, of necessity, universal and impersonal. Also, let us note, this most comprehensive of such precepts will, in the nature of the case, be incapable of derivation from any deeper-lying premise, without a circle in the proof. Thus the basic principle must be in some sense a priori.* But what will

* This topic could not be developed briefly. There is currently a considerable pother over it, and over the related question of any connection between indicative statements and "imperative" precepts. With respect to any who would dispute the claim that there *are* imperatives which it is not possible rationally to repudiate, there is a suggestion which can be briefly made: If they did not implicitly claim that their own expressed conviction is intelligent and rational, and imperative to believe, their verbal formulation would be sound and fury, signifying nothing. Like Epimenides the Cretan, who asserted that all Cretans are liars, those who so deny imperatives commit themselves to a statement which, if believed, would rob their assertion itself of significance and frustrate any purpose in making it. That, we may call a "pragmatic contradiction."

A little more circumstantially, the following considerations may be suggested as pertinent.

The creature which is not driven by impulse but must sometimes make his own decisions, must also find it imperative to respect consistency—in concluding and believing, in purposing, and in doing. Principles of action (of decisions to do), like principles of thinking (of decisions as to fact, conclusions), are finally rooted in respect for consistency.

Decisions of action have their premises, as decisions of belief have their premises. Consistency concerns the relation between a decision and its premises, and, more widely, the relation of all accepted decisions—all convictions of justified believing and justified doing—among themselves. Complete consistency would be the complete integrity of a completely rational self.

A rule of decision is valid a priori if the repudiation of it would be self-contravening—a pragmatic contradiction. Such a non-repudiable principle is "pragmatically a priori." The broadest of imperatives, "Be consistent," exemplifies this matter. A accord with it and what will contravene it, are matters of empirical fact to be determined—what consequences the act will have, who will be affected by them, and whether for good or for ill. And on such points the judgment of the individual is as fallible as on any other matter of empirical fact. No doer, nor anybody else, can perfectly foresee all consequences of any contemplated act; nor can his judgment of the goodness or badness of those which he foresees be guaranteed. His right-mindedness—his intent to conform to whatever is dictated by principles of right—is his integrity, all-important to himself, and socially important as indicating a certain reliability of his conduct in general. But by itself such moral intent will not assure that what he chooses to do will be that right thing which should be done. Over and above the intent to adhere to fundamental moral principle, well-judged moral practice calls for far-reaching understanding of the ramified consequences of different ways of acting, as well as an enlightened sense of human values.

decision without intent to adhere to it would not be a genuine decision. But one who should adopt the decision, "Disregard consistency," would be deciding to disregard his decisions as soon as made. And adherence to *that* decision would require that it be promptly disregarded.

It is a further difficulty of concrete moral judgments that, due to the remoteness of the fundamental principle from the particular case, intermediate generalizations are needed to bridge the gap. And it is such subordinate precepts which are most familiar to us as "moral rules": "Tell no lies," "Pay your debts," "Keep your promises," "Do not steal," "Be charitable," "When in Rome, do as the Romans do." These are our maxims. They represent ways of acting which, as experience has taught us, have some measure of reliability as satisfying the requirements of the fundamental principle. But precepts which are thus specific and at the same time valid without exception are hard to come by. As we are aware in the case of those cited, they often conflict with one another in practice: if you are short of funds, it may not be possible, without stealing, to pay your debts; and it is difficult to be always kind and charitable without sometimes coloring the truth. Also any one of them will have its exceptions in extremis, of which our common sense will presumably advise us: it is better not to keep a promise if fulfillment of it will endanger a life. Our acceptance of such a precept is accompanied by implicit understanding that it applies "under ordinary circumstances" or "as a rule." Formulation of it as strictly universal would require so many qualifications of "if" and "but" and "unless"—and so many that we do not think of at the moment—as to be impracticable if not theoretically impossible. And sometimes we arrive at the case where specific rules fail us altogether, and we do not know just what is the right thing to do. At such a point, we have to fall back upon the ultimate principle itself, implemented by such judgment of the individual case and such wisdom of life as we can muster.

The particular point of relevance of all this to what we would consider here, is the plain implication that, while the roots of the moral sense must lie in something common to all men and significant of their native endowment, correct moral practice, like correct technological practice of any sort, or correct practice in an art, is something which has to be learned and developed through relevant experience. The native moral sense, like the native logical sense, calls for clarification and enhancement by the critical processes implicit in social living and common thinking, and may stand in need of social reinforcement. And concerning specific questions of moral conduct there is the same need to call upon accumulated social wisdom, and to submit the matter to the social criticism, that there is in any other department of man's continuing search for ways to the better life.

Moral wisdom is subject to the same slow maturation of rationality, and to the empirical learning of what ways of acting will conduce to human betterment and what will work against it which similarly characterizes other forms of learning. The morals of primitive peoples are relative to their undeveloped insight and to their ignorance, just as their primitive mathematical and physical lore, and their backward agricultural or medical practice, are relative to their ignorance. They have not learned any better. And our own morals, at the beginning of the Atomic Era, will—we shall hope—eventually appear as frustrated and relatively unsatisfactory as, e.g., the moral wisdom of the period of the Crusades looks to us now. We are trying with all our powers to find out the better way for human life, in a world in which the mores of different peoples remain variously unenlightened, and in various degrees irrational and perverse. At any given time and in any historical context, prevailing morals are relative to the stage of human development, just as prevailing science and technology are. And the hope for further moral progress is tied to that same working of the critical processes and of learning, and to the social inheritance of ideas, which likewise make for progress in science and technology and in our political and other social institutions.

Also the relation of the individual to the cultural ideas which his generation inherits, in his time and place, is much the same in any department of it. However, it is precisely here that we arrive at a most critical question concerning the social inheritance of ideas and the working of it for progressive human betterment. And if what is said above should have appeared to elevate conformity as the highest of the social virtues, then on that point it will need correction. Without the social transmission of ideas there could be no civilization and no continuing progress—in science or technology or in morals. But if ideas so preserved should become authoritative in the sense of being uncriticizable by those who so acquire them, then at that point progress would be arrested. Not only is the liberty of thought essential to personality, and one of those highest goods which set the goals of human life, but in addition to any such natural-right sanction there is an indispensable social utility in the preservation of individual freedom of dissent.

There can be no item of learning, and nothing in any social consensus reached, which should not originate in individual minds, reflecting their diversities and that experimentalism which characterizes independent thinking. The social order is the main selecting and preserving agency. But without the freedom of private judgment—often dissident to tradition—there would be no intellectual innovation, and progress would dry up at the source.

There is a biological sanction even. We are not social insects whose communal solidarity represents an automatic and instinctive adjustment of individual behavior to the social needs. If we were, then, as was earlier pointed out, the history of humanity would show progress only through biological modification of the organism. And that is the very antithesis of the story of mankind as progressing through the agency of accumulated learning, socially transmitted and preserved. It is doubtful that free thought and dissident opinion *could* be rooted out, while the human animal remains intelligent. But if any really monolithic human society could be achieved, then it must mean the death of civilization, if not of the race; the freezing of the social order in some insect-like perfection of adjustment of the individual to the social status quo.

Human society, being built upon intelligence and rationality, and not upon instinct and contagious feeling and impulse, can continue to progress only by the preservation of individual liberties in thought and action. It capitalizes upon individual differences of propensity and aptitude and free choice, and prospers by achieving harmony in variety and the accommodation of diverse interests and aims; not by fitting individuals to a Procrustean bed of common attitude and opinion. In this, human society is the counterpart of the human individual himself, who likewise achieves his integrity and his self-realization by attaining consistency in the pattern of his purposes and the harmonious accommodation of interests which are diverse. Human good, whether in the individual life or in the social order, is achieved as the ordered relationship of multiple ingredients; as the enrichment of life, and not by reduction of it to any common denominator.

The dependence of continuing social progress upon the free initiative of individuals and their liberty of thought and communication, is pervasive of all aspects of any social order. And it is on this point that one civilization may differ most notably from another. Free societies progress; and those in which critical thinking is relatively suppressed must inevitably be retarded in like measure. Peculiarly this must be true with respect to those ideas which are moral in significance; because moral judgments, along with other modes of critical judgment attributable to rationality, are those which finally are determinative for the control and direction of deliberate activities in general. The particular point to be observed here, is that not only does the factor of social mores operate to accelerate or to retard the progress of a civilization in other departments of it, but that accepted mores operate to promote or to retard *moral* progress. The effective moral tradition includes those dominant attitudes and practices which touch, and foster or repress, the free working of the critical process *as directed upon prevailing mores themselves.* Thus accepted mores may tend to prohibit their own alteration and to perpetuate themselves unchanged; or they may permit and provide for their own critical reconsideration and possible improvement. The moral tradition of a people, as bearing on this point, must plainly be the most vitally important aspect of its civilization and the most decisive for its destiny in history. It must most deeply affect the question whether the social inheritance of ideas will, in this civilization, exercise that function by which it works for human betterment, or will cease to exercise it and become instead the root of stagnation and arrested development.

This is, of course, the point on which the prevailing tradition of Western civilization would distinguish itself most basically from any other. And we do well to recognize that this is, at one and the same time, the most deeply moral of all moral questions and that question the answer to which is most critically important for the future of mankind.

We must admit the moral factors as validly controlling if there is to be justification of anything human. Without the primacy of moral principle, there could be no right or wrong as between us and the social order we would defend, and any who would seek to displace and destroy our cherished institutions. Nor would there otherwise be a valid ground for the adjudication of any social policy, or criterion for our attempts to improve it, or any valid ends for us to aim at in the heritage which we would leave our children. All these would be merely things as they are, and as they will become, by the confluence of circumstances, the accidents of history, the chance equilibrium of opposing forces, or by the connivings of persons and parties each striving to have its own arbitrary way. Either the historic process in which we find ourselves involved is just the boiling up of its own particular kind of brew, and we float momentarily on the surface of it, or there is a power operative in human history which makes for the right and the good, and we have our privilege of participation and a valid end toward which to move. But whatever should be our confidence, or lack of it, in the attainment by men of the goals which represent their common aims, we still have no alternative but to conduct ourselves on the assumption of their validity and the possibility of their furtherance. Otherwise the common vocation of man would lack significance.

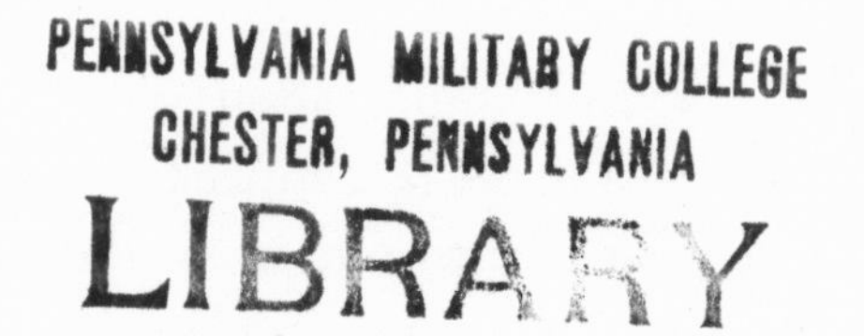

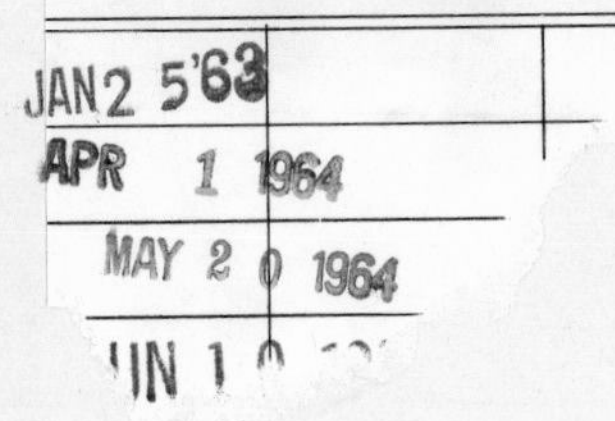